Written by

A N D

We have a bond that spans a lifetime.

There are things we'll always want to remember, things we admire about each other, and things we have only said secretly in our own hearts. Let's share them all inside these pages, where we'll get to know each other even better. I'll fill out the pages on the left while you fill out the pages on the right. It'll be a way that we can appreciate and celebrate the unique link between us. After all, our connection to each other is something only you and I can describe, together.

AS A KID, I USED TO THINK YOU...

Becoming your mom was...

WHEN I WAS LITTLE, I WANTED TO BE

WHEN I GREW UP.

SOMEONE I ADMIRED WAS

BECAUSE...

When I was little, I wanted to be

when I grew up.

Someone I admired was

       because... _____

_____

_____

_____

_____

_____

_____

_____

_____

MY FAVORITE BOOK GROWING UP...

_____

_____

_____

_____

_____

MY FAVORITE CHILDHOOD GAME WE PLAYED TOGETHER...

_____

_____

_____

_____

_____

A SONG THAT REMINDS ME OF MY CHILDHOOD...

_____

_____

_____

_____

_____

One of my favorite things about you...

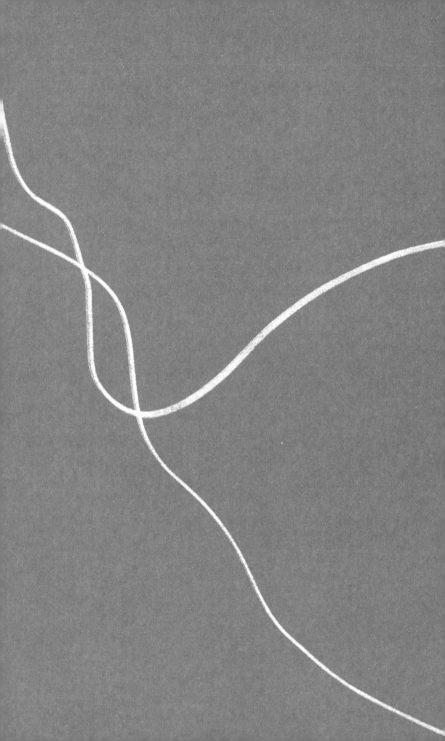

*Family faces are magic mirrors.
Looking at people who belong to us, we
see the past, present, and future.*

GAIL LUMET BUCKLEY

WHEN I WAS LITTLE, I LOVED IT WHEN YOU…

_____

_____

_____

_____

_____

_____

_____

_____

_____

_____

_____

_____

_____

_____

_____

_____

_____

_____

When you were little, I loved when we...

MY FAVORITE HOLIDAY GROWING UP WAS...

_____

_____

_____

_____

_____

WE WOULD CELEBRATE BY...

_____

_____

_____

_____

_____

AND WE'D ALWAYS...

_____

_____

_____

_____

_____

The year your favorite holiday stands out to me was...

_____

_____

_____

_____

_____

_____

_____

_____

_____

_____

_____

_____

_____

_____

_____

_____

_____

_____

GROWING UP, IT DROVE ME CRAZY WHEN YOU...

_____

_____

_____

_____

_____

_____

_____

_____

BUT NOW I RECOGNIZE YOU DID IT BECAUSE...

_____

_____

_____

_____

_____

_____

_____

_____

_____

As you were growing up, I never stopped loving you.
Even when we disagreed, I would...

When you look at your life, the greatest happinesses are family happinesses.

|

JOYCE BROTHERS

A NICKNAME YOU GAVE ME...

A WORD OR JOKE ONLY OUR FAMILY WOULD UNDERSTAND...

A WORD THAT BEST DESCRIBES OUR FAMILY'S PERSONALITY...

When you arrived, you created a brand-new family.
You changed everything by...

_____

_____

_____

_____

_____

_____

_____

_____

_____

_____

_____

_____

_____

_____

_____

_____

_____

ONE WAY YOU AND I ARE ALIKE...

AND ONE WAY WE ARE DIFFERENT...

I love that we share this in common...

_____

_____

_____

_____

_____

_____

_____

And I'm in awe how differently we...

_____

_____

_____

_____

_____

_____

_____

_____

YOU'VE SUPPORTED ME IN SO MANY WAYS. ONE THING
YOU DID FOR ME THAT I WILL NEVER FORGET...

You've helped me in so many ways. One thing you did for me...

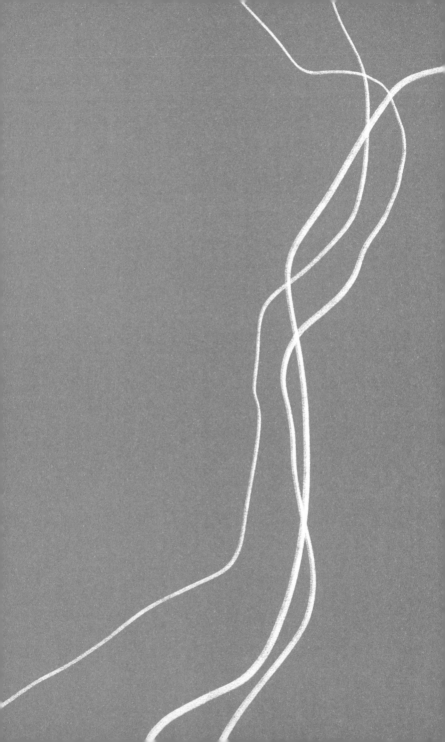

How strange, exciting and miraculous that we can change each other so much, love each other so much...

|

LAURIE ANDERSON

SOME THINGS I CONSIDER OUR FAMILY HEIRLOOMS...

ONE OF MY FAVORITES IS

BECAUSE...

ONE OBJECT THAT ALWAYS REMINDS ME OF YOU IS

One family keepsake that is special to me is

_____

       because... _____

_____

_____

_____

_____

_____

_____

_____

A memento from your childhood that I adore is

_____

A MEMORY I HAVE OF MY GRANDPARENTS...

A STORY I'VE HEARD ABOUT MY GRANDPARENTS...

A trait you share with your grandparents...

_____

_____

_____

_____

_____

_____

_____

_____

Your great-grandparents were...

_____

_____

_____

_____

_____

_____

_____

_____

_____

THANK YOU FOR ALWAYS BELIEVING IN ME.
YOU ENCOURAGE ME TO...

You make life richer, happier, and brighter.
Because of who you are, you inspire me to...

_____

_____

_____

_____

_____

_____

_____

_____

_____

_____

_____

_____

_____

_____

_____

_____

_____

_____

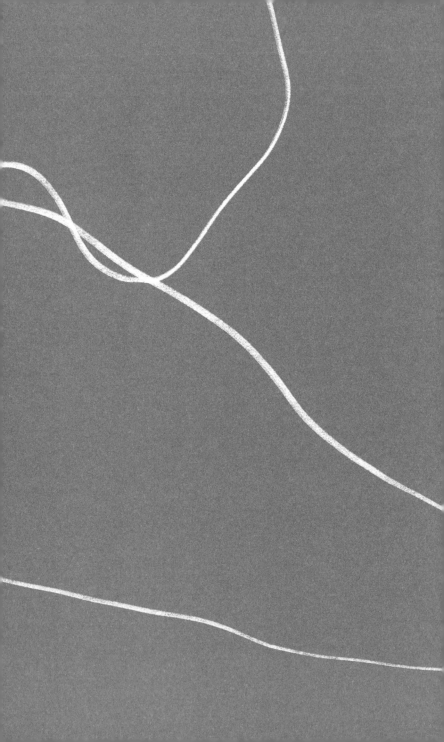

My heart gives thanks...

|

WILLIAM S. BRAITHWAITE

YOU'VE GIVEN ME SO MUCH IN SO MANY WAYS. HERE ARE
JUST A FEW THINGS I'M GRATEFUL FOR...

THANKS TO YOU, I...

I MAY NOT HAVE SAID THANK YOU AS OFTEN AS I COULD,
BUT I WANT YOU TO KNOW THAT...

Having you in my life has given me so much.
I'm grateful for you because...

_____

_____

_____

_____

_____

_____

_____

_____

_____

_____

_____

_____

_____

_____

_____

_____

_____

_____

YOU'VE HELPED MORE THAN JUST ME. HERE ARE
SOME WAYS I SEE YOU HELP OTHERS...

I love witnessing what a good person you've become,
like when you...

_____

_____

_____

_____

_____

_____

_____

_____

_____

_____

_____

_____

_____

_____

_____

_____

_____

DID YOU KNOW I'M PROUD OF YOU? I AM. AND HERE'S WHY...

_____

_____

_____

_____

_____

_____

_____

_____

_____

_____

_____

_____

_____

_____

_____

_____

I want you to know how proud I am of you. Here's why...

_____

_____

_____

_____

_____

_____

_____

_____

_____

_____

_____

_____

_____

_____

_____

_____

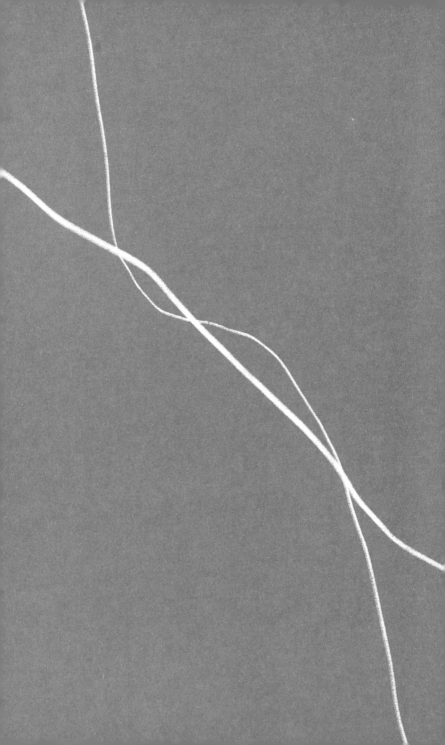

What greater thing is there for human souls than to feel that they are joined for life—to be with each other in silent unspeakable memories.

|

GEORGE ELIOT

ONE PLACE THAT REMINDS ME OF YOU IS...

YOU'VE LED ME ON LOTS OF ADVENTURES. HERE ARE SOME
OF MY FAVORITE PLACES WE'VE BEEN TO TOGETHER...

IF WE WENT ON A TRIP TODAY, JUST THE TWO OF US,
WE COULD...

A place I'd love to go with you sometime is

because...

YOU INSPIRE ME BY...

_____

_____

_____

_____

_____

_____

_____

_____

_____

_____

_____

_____

_____

_____

_____

_____

_____

It's incredible how you aren't afraid to...

SOMETHING YOU'VE TAUGHT ME THAT WILL
STAY WITH ME FOREVER...

_____

_____

_____

_____

_____

_____

_____

_____

_____

_____

_____

_____

_____

_____

_____

_____

And you've taught me...

Love is to love someone for who they are,
who they were, and who they will be.

|

CHRIS MOORE

A FEW WORDS I'D USE TO DESCRIBE YOU TO OTHERS...

AND IF I HAD TO CHOOSE ONE WORD TO DESCRIBE YOU, IT'D BE

If I were to describe you in a few words, they'd be...

_____

_____

_____

_____

_____

_____

_____

And if I had to choose one word to describe you, it'd be

ONE WISH I HAVE FOR YOU...

One wish I have for you...

_____

_____

_____

_____

_____

_____

_____

_____

_____

_____

_____

_____

_____

_____

_____

_____

I SEE YOUR LOVE EVERYWHERE. THINGS THAT ALWAYS
REMIND ME OF YOU ARE...

WHEN I THINK OF YOU, I FEEL...

I carry you with me wherever I go. Things that always remind me of you are...

_____

_____

_____

_____

_____

_____

_____

When I think of you, I feel...

_____

_____

_____

_____

_____

_____

_____

Happiness was made to be shared.

|

JEAN RACINE

ONE THING I'VE NEVER TOLD YOU BEFORE...

One thing I've never told you before...

BECAUSE OF YOU, I'VE REALIZED THAT THE MOST
IMPORTANT THINGS IN LIFE ARE...

Because of you, I've discovered that...

COMPENDIUM®

live inspired

With special thanks to the entire Compendium family.

CREDITS:

Written by: Miriam Hathaway
Designed by: Heidi Dyer
Edited by: Kristin Eade

ISBN: 978-1-946873-82-8

1st printing. Printed in China with soy inks.